The Art and Sensuality of Brazilian Zouk Dancing

Marie Alonzo Snyder

The Larry Czerwonka Company, LLC
Hilo, Hawai'i

First Edition — January 2016

Published by: The Larry Czerwonka Company, LLC
http://czerwonkapublishing.com

Printed in the United States of America

Cover painting "This is just the beginning" by Stephanie Bolton

Photograph on back cover by Elliot Gordon

ISBN: 0692608656
ISBN-13: 978-0692608654

Dedicated to my loving parents

The Art and Sensuality of Brazilian Zouk Dancing

1 BRIEF HISTORY OF BRAZILIAN ZOUK

The word Zouk is Creole for "party."

3 ZOUK BEGINNINGS IN THE USA

Only in the last three years did the USA see a momentous interest and growth in Zouk.

5 ONE DANCE: TWO STYLES AND NEW WAVES

Within the Brazilian Zouk or Zouk Lambada spectrum there are two distinct schools: Rio Style Zouk, also known as ZoukLove, and Porto Seguro Style Zouk, also known as LambaZouk. Rio Style as the name suggests, was developed in the iconic urban and beach setting of Rio de Janeiro.

7 ZOUK RELATIVES

As any new dance that is still growing and evolving, it will be subject to all the influences that surrounds it. I can speak only for the Zouk that is developing in the Big Island of Hawai'i. This is the largest island in the chain of islands in the State of Hawai'i, big enough for all seven of the other islands to fit within it.

9 FUNDAMENTAL COMPONENTS FOR DANCING ZOUK

Based on my training and experience as a professional dancer, choreographer, and teacher for the last three decades, I have come to the conclusion that there are three fundamental components that are key to Zouk technique and an understanding of the dance.

Table of Contents

21 ETIQUETTE AND INCIDENTALS OF THE DANCE

The styles of clothing worn at Zouk socials, run a gamut. In general it is very relaxed and casual. Ladies can wear jeans with a cropped top shirt, a blouse, leggings, a flowing skirt or dress, shorts, flats, heels, sneakers or at times barefoot. Hair is mostly worn down as it is an accessory for some as they dance.

Juliati

Feather/Pena Earrings
(*photo by Juliati Photography*)

Table of Contents

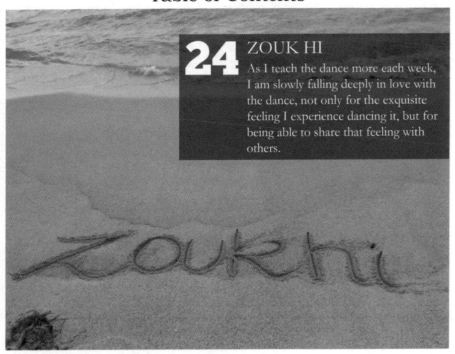

PREFACE

So I arrived in Kona, Hawai'i on November 17, 2014, leaving a life of over 33 years on the East Coast. I was called to this beautiful island, and Pele has cast a spell on my family and me as we are in love with Pele's home. I filled the island with Zouk and got the "party" dancing by the second week of my arrival. What just began with only one eager, lovely Zouk goddess in training, has now become a Heaven of gods and goddesses enjoying the passionate music, the sensual movements, and the delicious connection that Zouk offers.

Why a book on Brazilian Zouk dancing? Well, why not? I have been dancing it for over five years, and still there are so many people who do not know what it is, or have been turned off by some of the over-sexualized aesthetics, or all the sensationalized hair whipping, or have even misunderstood it for Zumba. There is only one book published in Spain on the dance, and I wanted to make sure that there was a way to educate people. There are blogs, articles, links to websites, radio stations, Facebook groups, and pages, but they are all for those who already know what Zouk is. But there is a dearth of literature for those who would want to read about it and understand what this whole hype or dance fad is all about. Indeed Zouk has been more readily passed from person to person through the actual experience and via social media. So I wrote this book from my perspective as a teacher and dancer of Zouk, but who has also been a professional modern dancer for over three decades, who fell in love with this social dance slowly, but deeply.

It is my hope that this book will educate the reader about this beautiful and deliciously sensual social dance that is growing in popularity all over the world and especially here in the USA. This will be the first book on Zouk published in the USA, and hopefully many more will be written to honor this dance and give it the respect and appreciation that it deserves.

Acknowledgement

First I want to thank my family: to Kirk, who has been so supportive of all my crazy dance projects for over 29 years, and to Gregory and Jonathan, who have come to accept their mother's passion for dance with so much love and encouragement.

To my first reader and editor, Elizabeth Madden Zibman, novelist, author, professor of English and friend, whose poems have continually inspired me not only to choreograph, but also to explore the many awesome possibilities that life has to offer, thank you and God bless you.

So grateful to my friends, dancers, non-dancers who continue to cheer, encourage, inspire, and bring out the best in me. There are too many here to list: Linda Mannheim, Christine Colosimo, Debra Keller, Fara Lindsay, Danielle Mondi, Karen Palowitch, Eri Millrod, Tamir Yardenne, Cynthia Bond Perry, Loren Bucek, Rina Corpus, Shelby Joy Cole, Stephanie Bolton, Tianna Peters, Peter Vancsa, Nagisa McClaren, Jill Jachera, Angel Umbach, Julie Ziemelis, Amy Ferris and all my Zouk students in the Big Island who have welcomed me with aloha into their community.

Last but not least, a big thank you to all my Zouk teachers who have helped me become the dancer and teacher that I am today: Jeremey Adam Rey, Solange Dias, Hisako Izutsu, Kim Rottier, Henry velandia (Ry'el), Larissa Thayanne, Evelyn Magyari, Xandi Liberato, Ian Pacheco, Ronny Dutra, K-yo Victor, Juni Shimitzu, Cledson Gomes, Daniela Pascual, Sofie Torris, Rodrigo Ramalho and Getulio Ramalho, and all the other amazing and generous teachers at congresses and festivals with whom I had the honor to take part in their classes.

(photo by James DeSalvo)

Brief History of Brazilian Zouk

The word Zouk is Creole for "party." Indeed, dancing Brazilian Zouk fills your heart with joy, the joy of connecting with another person, the joy of sharing the song being played, and the joy of moving one's body for those special four to five minutes of your life. But the word Zouk is also a particular social dance and rhythm found originally in the islands of Guadalupe, Martinique, and Haiti. So how did Brazil appropriate the word to name the growing social dance of the 21st century as described by Nicholas Bamboo of Zouk Nation (www.zouknation.com)?

Kim Rottier of Zouk, NY, (www.zoukny.com) offers a thorough historical development of the dance through the evolution of Zouk music bands. Beginning from the Kadans (creole for cadence) music from Haiti in the 1960's, which was further developed in Guadalupe and Martinique by adding American rock, soul, and

West African rhythms. Zouk was evolving by fusing musical elements. Soon a band Kassav was formed spreading the Caribbean rhythms worldwide in the 1970's and 80's. With this new Zouk music gaining popularity, it gradually replaced Brazilian Lambada music for Lambada dancers in Brazil.

Lambada was a Brazilian partner dance most popular in the 1980's. It was known for its close contact partnering and known also as the "forbidden dance" which soon faded in popularity. The word Lambada meaning the waves caused by a whipping

movement, reflects the dance's dynamic successional moves, many times involving also the dancer's hair as it carves the space with each head or torso circling movement.

This fusion of rhythm and movement was a cross pollination that gave birth to this beautiful and sensual dance that we now call Brazilian Zouk or Zouk Lambada, honoring both cultural roots. In this book, the dance will simply be referred to as Zouk as that has become its abbreviated name or nickname amongst those who know the dance, study the dance, and have seen the dance.

Frequently Asked Question: Is Zouk like Zumba?

Absolutely not. Zumba is a fun fitness workout using Latin rhythms and moves which could include also Zouk moves if the teacher is knowledgeable about the dance. Zouk is a sensual partner dance that comes from a fusion of cultural rhythms from the Caribbean and the evolved Lambada moves from Brazil.

(*Photo by MariTali Photography*)

Jeremey Adam Rey, who grew up listening and dancing to Haitian Zouk music with his Haitian father, is a leading Brazilian Zouk instructor in NYC and director of rawZouk. Here he is dancing with his Zouk dance partner, Shelby Joy Cole.

Zouk Beginnings in the USA

Only in the last three years did the USA see a momentous interest and growth in Zouk and accomplishments for the Zouk community. However, the history of Zouk in the USA started much earlier, according to Hisako Izutsu, a well-respected and internationally renowned Lamba-Zouk instructor for LambaZouk USA. The Zouk scene began about 17 years ago, with lots of turnovers of teachers and dancers. Basically it was a dance brought by transient individuals, who were generous to share the dance with others. It was also only recently that the people, who have been learning the dance, have taken a more active involvement in the community by promoting guest teachers, supporting workshops, and socials in New Jersey, New York, and Boston, and participating in the International Zouk Flash Mob for the last four years. Each individual's commitment in learning more and developing their skills has taken on a true passionate turn, in the recent three years, making NYC a growing and dynamic Zouk hub. In NYC, there are now weekly Zouk classes and socials at Solas, Stepping Out Studios, Pearl Studios, and DanceSport.

Aochan Nagamoto from Japan and Mari Hodges were the first couple, back in 1997, to introduce Zouk in NYC. Aochan learned Zouk from Gilson Damasco, Braz and Didi dos Santos while in Brazil learning Samba. Both Aochan and Mari then trained Hisako Izutsu and Juni Shimitzu. Mari stayed until 2002 and then she moved to Buenos Aires. Aochan remained until 2004, forming Tropical NY, which Juni took over in 2006. So for about two years, the Zouk community was dormant and continued simply by gathering together for private Zouk parties keeping the dance alive. In the meantime, also in 2006, Kim Rottier along with Pablo Schmoller, founded ZoukNY, an instrumental organization that has helped bring workshops and guest instructors to the U.S. Zouk scene, like Pedro Mesquita of Soul Zouk from 2007-2008.

In 2007, Nicholas Bamboo created Zouk Nation, a non-partisan group to promote both Brazilian Zouk and Zouk music. Through Zouk Nation, many events were organized: Brazilian Zouk Boat Cruises, participation in Dance Parade, weekly parties at Lava Gina, Zouk in Central Park, and the Brazilian Carnival at the 92nd Street Y in 2009. Zouk Nation's website (launched in 2009) has featured instructors,

Zouk sensuality with Getulio from Brazil and Hisa of LambaZouk USA
(Photo by Marie Di Raimondo)

recording artists, articles, and a directory of instructors. Other instructors who have contributed to the growth of Zouk in NY from 2007-2011 include: Aria Atai, Stephanie Batot, Kristina Melike, Garret English , Jeroen Van Weeghel, Ronny Dutra, Mike Farbrikant, Dennis Mook, Willem Engel, Nausha Hassankhan, Sarah Gibbons, Marcos Fonseca, Luciana Guinle and K-yo Victor.

Today one can take classes from the next generations of teachers. Juni's protégé, Jeremey Adam Rey of rawZouk brings a distinct Caribbean flavor to his Zouk teaching that reflects his Haitian heritage, along with his background in ballroom and salsa technique. With his partner and ballroom champion, Shelby Joy Cole, they offer private lessons and a rigorous 2-hour class every third Sunday before Las Chicas Locas social in NYC. At Stepping Out Studio, one can take Zenzouk classes with Henry velandia (Ry'el) of Zenzouk, a method of teaching various forms of Brazilian zouk through the use of elements, such as Earth Water, Fire, and Air. He teaches with his dance partner Jessica Lamdon. Level 1-3 classes with Kim Rottier and the faculty of ZoukNY are also offered at Pearl Studios.

Hisa Izutsu has been a strong leader in the LambaZouk style, who recently got certified to teach by Didi Dos Santos in Brazil. In 2014, Rodrigo Ramalho and Aline Cleto, from Brazil, shared their Zouk expertise while continuing their dance and acting training in NYC. In 2015 several visiting teachers like Ian Pacheco, Kamacho, Mafie Zouker, K-yo Victor, Getulio Ramalho, Charles Espinosa, Jefferson Dadinho, Leon Gordin, X-tine and Leonardo Bilia, offered special workshops or taught the pre-social lesson.

An event that helped change the Zouk landscape worldwide, promote Zouk in the USA, and recruit more dancers was the 2012 IZFM (International Zouk Flash Mob, now known as International Zouk Day) which attracted people to simply participate in a fun dance event, without realizing that soon, they would fall in love with the dance.

Additionally in 2013, Shani Mayer and Ivo Viera organized the first US Zouk Congress in Los Angeles, which began a new wave of Latin Festivals and Congresses that would include Zouk workshops. Later that year, Kim Rottier and Henry velandia (Ry'el), organized the first Fall For Zouk, a 3-day festival of workshops, performances, and social dancing in NYC, with local and International guest instructors. Even Honolulu organized a Dances of Love Festival that included Zouk, Bachata, and Kizomba. In 2014, DC, Miami, Seattle and Boston joined in by organizing successful events.

4

Frequently Asked Question:
Can Anyone Zouk?

YES! Anyone who loves to dance and wants to learn a new dance, who is committed in learning it correctly, who loves the music, who loves partner dancing, who loves the social interactions, and new friendships can dance Zouk. Kids can dance it. In fact, there is a father and daughter who have posted videos of them practicing keeping it age appropriate yet still with "ginga"(with flavor and soul). Middle age people 40 and up surely can enjoy it as much as the young people http://bit.ly/1TgkWwQ. Seated dancers in wheelchairs have also benefitted from the fluid upper torso movement, and the sensuality of the dance making them feel free. Here is an interview done by Zouk Nation on dancing with dancers in wheelchairs. http://bit.ly/1QKacsM

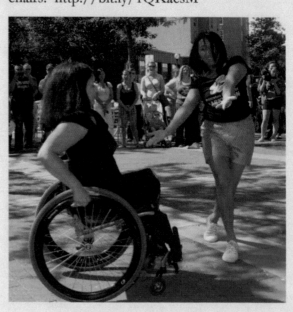

"Zouk For All" with Luz and me in Princeton, NJ
(Photo by Elliot Gordon)

One Dance: Two Styles and New Waves

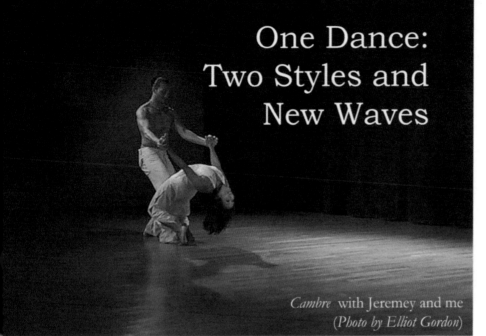

Cambre with Jeremey and me
(*Photo by Elliot Gordon*)

Within the Brazilian Zouk or Zouk Lambada spectrum there are two distinct schools: Rio Style Zouk, also known as ZoukLove, and Porto Seguro Style Zouk, also known as LambaZouk. Rio Style as the name suggests, was developed in the iconic urban and beach setting of Rio de Janeiro. Porto Seguro Style on the other hand, reflects the vibrant tropical beach town and birthplace of Lambada. Both are equally valuable to the growth of the Zouk community in Brazil and all over the world.

The Porto Seguro style or LambaZouk has kept the faster Caribbean version of the music with the characteristic high energy (*energia*) and feel good attitude (*alegria*), as well as the circular smooth moves and pronounced hip movements. Didi and Braz do Santos are brothers from Porto Seguro who danced and toured with music band Kaoma, while developing the Lambada dance. Eventually they became instrumental in creating the distinct moves of LambaZouk, specifically the head moves that are often seen in the dancing: head circles (*Cabeca/Boneca*) Hair whip/flick movements (*Chicote*) and Back arches and dips (*Cambre*).

The Rio Style or Zouk Love used slower music allowing a lot of the ebb and flow characteristic of the dance. In the 1990's as Lambada was fading in popularity, Adilio Porto and Renata Peçanha were instrumental in formulating basic moves like the forward and back basic move (*paso basico*), the transitional pivot step (*lateral/infinity*) and the travelling turn pattern (*bonus/boomerang/frisbee*). Adilio Porto is one of the most influential Brazilian dancers and teachers who spread Zouk all over Brazil, but also around the world. Renata Peçanha is renowned as the "Queen of Zouk Lambada" and is the director of an esteemed dance academy in Rio de Janeiro, which specializes in Zouk Lambada.

Just like modern dance, Zouk takes on the style, the philosophy, the training, and dance techniques of the teacher leading the class. As a very young dance, it has been evolving, creating an aesthetic influenced by music, one's creative vision, current dance trends, and simply the cross pollination that transpires at all these congresses and festivals around the world.

A new wave of Zouk is the Neo-Zouk, which was influenced with the coming of Remixes of contemporary songs by DJs like Mafie Zouker. With his philosophy, you get in and out of the music's rhythm, allowing a flow that is based on the dancers' feel for the music, which is necessary as contact improvisation (see Chapter 8) was added as another element in Zouk dancing. Some offshoots are FlowZouk, which incorporates more physical contact, reactive following and more contained partnering; Soul Zouk, on the other hand, is a teaching methodology based on Four Concepts (comfort, contact, leading, and joy); while R'n'B Zouk, uses Hip-hop and R&B music, with isolations and sharper and less expansive moves.

Transcending age with Nagisa and Manny both studying with Zenzouk in the NYC rain
(Photo by SCPhotography - Steven Colon)

Frequently Asked Question:
What is the difference in rhythm between RioZouk and LambaZouk?

Rio Zouk's rhythm in an 8 count musical phrase would be: slow (1-2) quick (3) quick (4) slow (5-6) quick (7) quick (8) - Não Me Toca by Anselmo Ralph.

LambaZouk's on the other hand is the reverse: quick (1) quick (2) Slow (3-4) quick (5) quick (6) Slow (7-8). És a Minha Doçura by Irmãos Verdades

Although subtle, there is a distinct difference in the tempos, breaks, transitions, accents, and aesthetics because the music dictates the dynamics of each of these styles.

Zouk Relatives

As any new dance that is still growing and evolving, it will be subject to all the influences that surrounds it. I can speak only for the Zouk that is developing in the Big Island of Hawai'i. This is the largest island in the chain of islands in the State of Hawai'i, big enough for all the other seven islands (Oahu, Maui, Kauai, Lanai, Molokai, Niihau, and Kahoolawe) to fit in. With the size approximately of the State of Connecticut and a growing population of 189,191 (2012 Census), Zouk has become a popular partner dance that many are discovering and enjoying.

With classes from three people up to twenty-four—as a teacher, I can't complain, that is a lot I can't complain, that is a lot for this island. When Master Teacher, Jeremey Adam Rey, was here for the first Zouk-ation dance intensive in the Big Island, the last workshop had 40 people at the Honoka'a People's Theatre, and many others came to observe the class. You can find a lesson for only $5 in downtown Kona every Tuesday at Daylight Mind Coffee Company and hoping to find a venue to have only Zouk once a month! Plus there are progressive series of classes for those who want to be more challenged and cover the ZOUK HI syllabus, in Heaven at Mauna Lea Manor Studio, in Holualoa. On Fridays, there are classes in the northern town of Waimea, at the Green Church, and the University of Hawai'i in Hilo offers intensive workshops.

Zouk's beauty is that you can bring your own style, or create your own style by fusing other dance styles and genre. Lately there has been a great development between West Coast Swing and Zouk, as they have been presented together at some special congresses like Vision Dance Encounter in Toronto, Canada, in 2014, and at the recent New York Fall For Zouk, and at the upcoming West Coast Swing and Zouk championship in Australia. These events will spur more interest to explore this fusion. As for me, I had a fantastic dance at a West Coast Swing social here in Kona dancing with Warren D'Aquin, a long time West Coast dancer and now part-time dance instructor, when not traveling or scuba diving around the world. So there is a wonderful opportunity for cross-pollination here in the island that is not only for flowers!

Another cousin of Zouk and growing in popularity is Kizomba, also known as African Tango. Kizomba is a partner dance from Angola, West Africa, and it has become very popular in Portugal and France. Both Zouk and Kizomba dances can use similar music at times, both have ties to African rhythms, and both have been presented

"The **beauty** of Zouk is that you can **create** your own **style.**"

in numerous Congresses and Festivals to widen the pool of participants to the events.

Belly dancing or Middle Eastern dance is also perhaps a more distant cousin. Some music can be shared if the thoom chik chik (Chapter 6) can be heard at the right tempo and many of the embellishments and torso isolations can be applied to one's Zouk dancing. Indeed Juni Izutsu, Zouk teacher in NY, who is also a skilled belly dancer, suggested it as a way to help one's Zouk dancing!

Another even more distant relative to Zouk is Pole dancing. A lot of Zouk music is quite suitable to pole dancing and many Zouk body isolations, moves, and hair tossing can be applied to pole routines. And indeed, I am in the process of creating a class for pole dancers that incorporates the sensuality and body moves in Zouk.

Last but not least, with Hula dancing in the Island, I wonder what influences it will have on my Zouk dancing. Some beautiful original Mele songs created for Hula, as well as local Jawaiian music are quite "Zoukable" and may contribute to the developing dance style in the island, starting another creative journey for me.

Frequently Asked Question:
How do I know who is a good teacher?

Simply try one of the classes to see if the teacher works for you. If you come out of the class having a confident understanding of the concepts/movements/techniques, then you're in the right place. You'll also want to feel inspired and encouraged by the teacher as she/he points out any weaknesses. You never want to feel discouraged or belittled. As Charles F. Glassman says, "A genuine teacher does not seek to impress you with their greatness, but instead to impress upon you that you possess the skills to discover your own."

Also, you may want to inquire about the teacher's background. Having a trained dancer, who has experience teaching dance in general, may offer a more structured, concise class with articulate instructions. You may also want to ask what kind of Zouk is being taught, so that you do not come with preconceived assumptions. In addition, there is a difference in teaching technique and in teaching styling, and that has to be clear. As the first is fundamental for progression and mastering CIA (see Chapter 5), and the latter is an embellishment with flourishes that are meant to inspire and express the personal style of the dancer.

(photo by Bruno Kongawoin)

Fundamental Components for Dancing Zouk

Based on my training and my experience as a professional dancer, choreographer, and teacher for the last three decades, I have come to the conclusion that there are three fundamental components that are key to Zouk technique and understanding of the dance. Those elements are best understood by the acronym CIA, for Connection, Intention, and Attention.

Connection: the connection to one's partner and thus, the aspect of partnering and trust/vulnerability.

Intention: the intention of each move that one makes (leading or following), and thus the aspect of physicality.

Attention: the attention to the music's phrasing and rhythms, and thus the aspect of musicality.

Therefore, part of studying Zouk is not only learning steps, but also learning what it means to partner with clarity and generosity, as well as being present and aware of one's body movement, in addition to listening and interpreting the music together.

First, one great way to establish that initial connection is to look at your partner and breathe together, and let the moment connect you organically and effortlessly. This I have learned from an enlightening Zouk workshop "How to get from good to great" by a teacher from the Netherlands, Kwok Won. Additionally, Zouk Master Teacher from Brazil, Marcelo Grangeiro, also emphasized the importance of maintaining the collarbone visual connection, to stay connected in the dance. And last, I encourage the leads to mold their moves to the shift of the follower's weight, to help with the direction of the body and the Connection.

Secondly, as soon as one makes contact, wait and listen to the lead, as instructed by MZouk Master Teacher, Daniel Estevez Lopez from Barcelona, at a workshop during the London ZoukFest 2014. That way there is no unnecessary back-leading assumptions of what may come next, or guessing of the move. This method allows the lead to be clear in his/her leading techniques, and ultimately gives him/her creative opportunities. By simply waiting and listening, the follower creates a trust in the partnership and the movements, for both have meaning and Intention.

Thirdly, as follower and leader move with connection and intention, the music finally becomes the "third" partner in the dance bringing the dancers together as one with the music. Zouk instructor, Jeremey Adam Rey, at the Charlotte Latin Invitational in 2014, informed the class, that the lead dances with the music and that the follower becomes the tool through which the rhythms, the melody, the instruments, the phrasing, the accents, and the lyrics are interpreted and expressed together in the dance. Therefore, to create a memorable Zouk experience, a key ingredient is Attention to musicality.

Frequently Asked Question:
Does one have to have all three CIA mastered to make a dance successful?

Without applying these components and making it a habitual technique, it will be very hard to do complex patterns correctly. Remember, without connection, one can't do dips safely; without intention, the moves will not have the power and clarity to look effortless and graceful; without attention to the music and rhythms, the dance will simply become a physical drill and not an expressive and memorable moment for the couple.

Hug me if you Zouk – 2015 Zouk HI T-Shirt

Four Rhythmic Patterns in Zouk

There are four rhythmic patterns in Zouk dancing, which help to building a connection to the music and with one's partner. Jeremey Adam Rey of rawZouk NYC has been teaching Zouk with this key component. For the chapter, "Thoom chik chik" will be used for the sound of the Zouk rhythms. Thoom having the same musical value to a set of chik chik.

The first rhythmic pattern is the down beat, Thoom _ _ Thoom _ _ or Slow _ _ Slow _ _

The second rhythmic pattern is double time, Thoom Thoom Thoom Thoom – or Slow Slow Slow Slow

The third rhythmic pattern is the regular Rio Zouk rhythm Thoom chik chik Thoom chik chik or Slow quick quick Slow quick quick

The fourth rhythmic pattern is similar to the third but it is syncopated. (Syncompation is a shift of rhythmic accents or a disturbance of regular rhythmic pattern). So now the first beat (thoom) is slightly shorter and the second beat (chik) is slightly longer thus both becoming equal in value. Sometimes to differentiate the regular Rio and the Syncopated, I sound it out as, pah pah chik.

Rhythmic Patterns in Brazilian Zouk Dancing
(Notation by Michaeloa Elam, conductor of Kona Chamber Orchestra)

It is very important to hear and understand these rhythmic patterns as it will become a solid foundation for the dance. It will make the dancing varied and in tune with the various instruments and rhythms that one can hear in a song. Additionally, it breaks the constant and possible monotony of Thoom chik chik, allowing a refreshing break rhythmically and physically.

The first rhythm can be used to do many of the various lead isolations: the "snake" or the "sway" or "body waves." And it is also a good tempo while trying to connect at the beginning of a dance.

The second rhythm allows a little more movement and travelling. By simply alternating steps from one foot to the other (similar to Merengue or Kizomba), one has the option of moving around in one spot or moving forward or back while doing a small body wave. The third rhythm is the regular Zouk rhythm used all the time to start moving through space.

The fourth rhythm allows seamless transitions by adding almost like a little lift on the first Thoom (or pah) which allows a quicker change of direction.

Frequently Asked Question:
How can I practice the 4 rhythmic patterns?

The best way is to listen to Zouk music a lot, either on Spotify, or at hipconaction.com, and clap each of the rhythmic patterns for one whole song, then all of them for one song, and repeat using your feet, stepping it out to mark each rhythmic pattern.

Performing a collaborative Zouk choreography with Zouk teacher Jermey Adam Rey @ West Windsor Arts Center, NJ
(*Photo by James De Salvo*)

Three Leading Techniques

There are three ways that one can lead in Zouk: Tactile, Tactile and Visual, and simply Visual.

(Photo by MariTali Photography)

(Photo by Frank White)

(Photo by Marie Di Raimóndo)

TACTILE

The Tactile lead is a physical connection. The leader gives physical cues to where he wants the follower to go. It is a very secure and clear lead that at times it is possible for the follower to simply close her eyes and enjoy the moves she is invited to do.

TACTILE AND VISUAL

The Tactile and Visual lead is perhaps what is mostly used in dancing Zouk. There is a physical connection and a visual cue to lead the follower toward a shift of weight (i.e. lunge before exit turn, or mirroring), space (i.e. tilt during a transition for *boneca* or a *diamond*), time (i.e. initiating a body wave) or body part contact (i.e. elbow, torso, chin, forehead). This Tactile and Visual technique is necessary especially when the leader wants to try something creative, unusual or unconventional, so this allows different ways for the follower to be sensitive to the new lead and in tuned with the changes.

VISUAL

The Visual lead is used when there is no physical contact, what in Zouk we call Wi-Fi moments. This is when the leader continues the lead without physically connecting with the follower. A heightened awareness and connection are necessary to make this work clearly and smoothly. One of the most common steps, when the follower is let go, is during the *soltinho* or *giros* (a step/thoom, pivot/chik shift/chik move, followed by a three step turn on the next thoom-chik-chik). This is done in a circle and allows some styling for both. The leaders may add some single or double turns with variations in arms, and followers may add some hip led turns, arm variations, or some playfulness with the hair or skirt. The most important part is for the follower to keep eye contact with the leader and to be receptive to the hand signals.

Checklist for the leaders as they are dancing:
Which arm is leading?
What is the direction of your move?
Where are you in rhythm for each step?

Checklist for followers as they are dancing:
Where do you feel the lead?
Where are you in relationship to the lead?
Where are you in rhythm?

Frequently Asked Question:
What do I do if the lead is off rhythm ?

1. Try to get him to rhythm by hijacking the move and slow it down or speed it up so that you get back to Thoom and SMILE.

2. Give the guy a chance to realize that he is off and most of the time he does, and he either stops or leads you into a body role and smiles ... so please SMILE back.

3. If all fails, then simply ignore the music and follow the leads and have fun styling as long as you keep following smoothly you both will have fun!

For all smile and thank your partner for the dance.

Zouk with Aloha
Shelby and Jeremey
(*Photo by MariTali Photography*)

Movement Techniques

Core Strength

The beauty about Zouk and what distinguishes it from other partner dancing is that it allows the body to explore different ranges of motion for both the leader and the follower, creating these wonderful moments of effortless ebb and flow of partnering. However, part of creating such an illusion is in part based on a strong core, articulate spine/torso, and use of breath.

The core in Zouk may not be so obvious, but, in fact, its strength will allow better partnering, better stamina for fast songs, and safer use of the spine and torso. As a certified Pilates instructor who has instructed many dancers, I recommend developing a strong core which is physically essential and an important part for any dancer from ballet to Flamenco, from modern to salsa, from hip hop to Zouk. Having a strong core does not necessarily mean a six pack or a totally flat belly, but what it means is that the person has an awareness and understanding of how to engage his or her core muscles: the abdominals, the glutes, the latissimus dorsi, and the spinalis.

Understanding what muscles to fire to stabilize a specific part of the body, in order to initiate the movement, and sustain it, and being able to change it at a rapid speed, is fundamental to building core strength. Pulling in the abdominals; engaging the glutes to keep the pelvis lifted and squared; drawing the shoulder blades down to imaginary back pockets; engaging the lats, as if one is carrying a purse under the armpits; keeping the neck long from the back as if someone were pulling the ears up to the ceiling, are all part of the preparations that the body makes in order to move efficiently and with control! It may seem like a lot to think about, but with practice the muscles will be conditioned to work correctly. The beginning warm-up in class, is a prime time to prepare the body from the inside out. Taking responsibility for one's body is key to optimum performance quality and stronger technique.

Breath

Articulating the spine is basically what makes Zouk so attractive to many and especially for a dancer in a wheelchair, because it adds a liberating feeling especially of the torso. The freedom that one feels comes from the use of the breath and its resulting movement of the spine and torso. Breath is important in dancing, and one needs to develop an awareness and control of the inhale and exhale while moving through space. Breath is movement and it becomes part of the dancing for the individual person and for the partnership. As a modern dancer I was attracted to Zouk because of its similar moves to modern dance techniques I have studied.

First, the notion of dancing Zouk with Aloha gives the dancers the opportunity to be present, breathe and connect. Indeed, in the Hawaiian language Aloha means love, affection, compassion, kindness, grace, charity, greeting, salutation, to love, to be fond of, to show kindess, to show affection, to venerate, to greet and to remember with affection. So the moment two people decide to dance with each other, you salute each other with an awareness of each other's breath. It is the moment when one exhales and surrender to each other's grace, kindness, compassion and generosity. And through this special partnership one shows the love for the dance and the fondness for the music. Zouk with aloha becomes a way to share a dance together with respect for each other, honoring the strengths and weaknesses of one another, to create a dance that will be remembered with affection. I wanted to apply that aloha into one's Zouk, especially in the beginning, not only as a greeting when the breath is synchronized and becomes one, but also as a way to connect physically, emotionally and spiritually for those four minutes of the song.

Isadora Duncan (1877-1927) is considered the pioneer of Modern dance. Her use of breath is natural and it follows the ebb and flow of the ocean waves and is initiated at the solar plexus. In Zouk, that is a helpful and concrete landmark as it allows one to keep the torso wide open, vulnerable, receptive, and generous as one moves. This stance helps with fluid transitions and promotes a posture that exudes a natural confidence in movement.

Martha Graham (1894-1990), the mother of American modern dance, is renowned for the use of breath that progresses to a contraction and release of the center of the body. In Zouk, it is important to understand how to use this technique, so that when we bend over or arch or dip or in complex transitions, i.e. in the "Diamond," one can become aware of how to use the breath, the contraction of the upper torso and release from the center. When the breath becomes part of the move, a total mindful physicality happens making one's dancing more organic with fewer affectations or mannerisms.

Body Articulations

Jose Limon (1908-1972) and Erick Hawkins (1917-1994) are Second generation modern dance masters. Limon worked with Doris Humphrey, from whom he developed the principle of weight, and fall and recovery, who also had his own company Jose Limon Dance Company. Hawkins was Martha Graham's first male dancer in her company, who later left, and began his company Erick Hawkins Dance Company, developing instead a gentle and free flow technique.

Jose Limon's successional technique where one body part leads and the rest follows is a great way to understand how to make each movement fluid in its articulation and for Zouk dancers to understand from where the movement initiates, from the head, from shoulder, from ribcage, from hip! The more articulate the body is, the more powerful and graceful the movement becomes.

Erick Hawkins technique of spiraling imagery from the feet to the head allows a Zouk dancer prepare and execute movements with a body that is fully integrated from bottom to the top. Understanding the full physicality of the body when one leads/follows any move that requires a turn, or circling or spinning will enhance the execution, making it more efficient and effortless.

Contact Improvisation

Last but not least, Contact Improvisation technique is widely used as one dances Zouk, especially in Neo-Zouk, Zouk Flow, Soul Zouk, and Mzouk styles. Contact improvisation is a postmodern dance technique that was started by Steve Paxton (b.1939) in the 1970's. It is based on seamless exchange of body weight, and the use of body contact to initiate and explore other spontaneous movement.

The concept of applying Contact Improvisation in Zouk was made apparent at a workshop taught by Kwok Wan, in NYC in 2012. It is also the technique used by Zouk teachers under the name of Neo-Zouk, Zouk Flow and Mzouk. Just like modern dance, Zouk takes on the style, the philosophy, and the training and dance techniques of the teacher who is teaching the dance. As a very young dance, Zouk has been evolving, creating new aesthetic influenced by music, one's creative vision and simply the cross pollination that transpires at all of these congresses and festivals around the world.

Frequently Asked Question:
How do I improve on all 3?

A Simple exercise that will help you become aware of your core, your spine articulation and your breath is a simple rolling down and up of your spine from a seated position with bent legs and arms gently resting under one's thighs. Sitting up straight, inhaling, pulling in the abdominals, engaging the glutes and then slowly rolling down, imprinting the tailbone, lower back, and ribs. Then exhaling as the shoulder blades touch the ground, and roll down through your upper back, and release the neck nice and long. And then reverse it, inhale, pull in abdominals and engage glutes, draw shoulders blades down and lift the head and round up, chest, ribs, and exhale roll through lower back and tail bone, and slowly lengthen the spine and ears up to the sky.

A simple improvisation exercise you can do by yourself is to come up with 30 moves in 30 seconds and none can be repeated, varying the parameters: focus on legs, or the back, low level, high level, travelling, stationary, sharp, curved etc… in the moment spontaneous moves and work toward a full minute. This will allow you to explore your range of movement, create new moves, and moving spontaneously with no right or wrong.

Introductory Steps

There is no substitute to learning a dance in person with a teacher who will correct, encourage and challenge you. But there are some fundamental moves that one can get started with while looking for a Zouk teacher or thinking about taking on this dance.

First Step is what is covered in Chapter 6, the 4 rhythms. Understanding how to use them in your dancing and hearing and interpreting the music, will make those 4 minutes a delightful and delicious experience for both.

Second step is the Basic step using rhythm 3 or 4. Leaders will always start with the Left foot going back on the *Thoom* and step Right Left on *chik chik* and then ready to step forward with Right on *Thoom* and step Left Right on *chik chik*. Follower's steps are the reverse, always starting with the Right foot going forward on the *Thoom* and step Left Right on chik chik and then ready to step back with Left on *Thoom* and step Right Left on *chik chik* When using rhythm 4 which is syncopated and the first *Thoom* is slightly shorter and the first *chik* slightly longer than in Rhythm 3, there is a natural lift of the body as one steps with rhythm 4.

Third step is the Leader's Lateral also known as Infinity. But lateral is a better name to describe the movement for both dancers. For the leader's Lateral, one steps laterally, to the Left side on thoom and step together R and step L in place (more styling can be done when CIA—see Chapter 4 on Connection Intention Attention—is mastered for this move) and then side step to the Right on *Thoom* and step together L and step R in place on *chik chik*.

Fourth Step is the follower's Lateral. One steps forward on Right foot on *Thoom* and then step L and pivot to the right shifting the weight on the Right foot on *chik chik*. Then this is simply repeated to the other side. It is called a Lateral as the pathway goes left to right, or right to left of the leader, who steps the opposite direction, creating this crisscross effect on the dance floor. Many refer to this movement of the follower also as the Infinity. The Lateral or Infinity is a step on its own, where the follower can be given the chance to style with her hair, hip, level change, foot embellishments, and accents. But it is also an important transitional step to understand as it is key in changing directions, leading to more complex steps, or traveling through space.

With all these moves it is important to let the hips go and feel free and sensual, and smile!

Frequently Asked Question:
Do I have to do all those head and hair moves if I do Zouk?

The answer NO! It is the responsibility of the follower to let the leader know that she or he is not comfortable or not ready or is injured. Most of the head and torso moves are done through the partner's lead. There are so many beautiful moves in Zouk where the hair whipping and flinging are not necessary and actually they have almost become a quick way to give the illusion of being an advanced dancer even though one is not. It has become so frequent that onlookers think Zouk is all about the hair-ography, making it less attractive to those who don't have long hair or whose bodies are no longer as limber or have a weak/injured neck!

(Photo by MariTali Photography)

19

Variations on the Dance Floor

There are two peculiar dance structures that can be found in Zouk dancing, both are quite entertaining and technically challenging especially for the lead.

The first variation is what I would call "stealing." Indeed this is when a man tries to literally steal the lady from the man dancing with her. It gets quite exciting as, at times, there is more than just one lead prowling, watching, circling the dancing couple, and waiting for those quick open moments when one can slip in between and continue with the dance without losing timing and rhythm. There is almost a primal feel to this characteristic variation that happens on the dance floor. It is spontaneous, playful, testosterone-driven, and energetic showmanship of stealing skills. As far as for the lady dancing with each of the men and being passed around, it can be an exquisite moment where all the focus is on her, while she enjoys the different leads while being taken cared by each of her partners.

The second variations that is just as vibrant, fun, and as playful is what I call "trio" or "trio plus." This is when the lead is dancing with more than one follower almost like a Zouk version of a threesome! It can be as many as two or more ladies at once. This is the moment where team work is important. It is simply about following the leader and being aware that there are others he is leading. For the follower, it is important to curb the styling so that all the followers are working as a team instead of trying to outdo each other and steal the attention. This is more of a group effort and enjoying this crazy ride while the lead is managing two or more ladies. Sometimes he is holding a lady in each hand, while there is one on a close embrace and one or more circulating around him as he exchanges ladies. This is all done while keeping the beat and rhythm. At times the man simply let's go of all the ladies and uses the Wi-Fi non-tactile technique to lead the big group. It becomes a spectacle of smiles and laughter, team work at its best and perhaps a test of leading skills and crowd management for any lead.

Last but not least, is the celebratory circle dance. This variation is used to celebrate birthdays or to welcome a guest teacher or to say goodbye. The celebrant whether male or female remains in the center while encircled by others who simply take turns leading or following. It is more laid back then a "stealing" since each person wants to give a chance to everybody in the circle to dance with the celebrant.

Etiquette and Incidentals of the Dance

Hygiene: Since dance is a physical activity where you not only sweat but are in close contact with others who are sweating, it is imperative that each dancer takes care of her or his hygiene for the benefit of all. You definitely do not want people to avoid dancing with you because you are too sweaty or starting to expel some unsavory bodily fragrance.

A top Zouk teacher at the beginning of a workshop wisely reminded students of some dance etiquette at socials for both ladies and gentlemen: Bring extra clothing to change to (especially men 3 to 8 T-shirts); use and bring deodorant; chew some gum or mints to keep the breath fresh and a towel to dry off the sweat profusely oozing out after each dance.

Fashion: The styles of clothing worn at Zouk socials, run a gamut. In general it is very relaxed and casual. Ladies can wear jeans with a cropped top shirt, a blouse, leggings, a flowing skirt or dress, shorts, flats, heels, sneakers or at times barefoot. Hair is mostly worn down as it is an accessory for some as they dance. But my favorite accessory are the single feather earrings that Hisako sells and my latest

fashion fad are Hawaiian plumeria and beads arm bracelet or metallic temporary tattoos. The guys simply wear whatever they feel comfortable in, T-shirt and jeans or sweats or baggy shorts with sneakers. Men also like to grow their hair long and some like to wear a shell arm bracelet.

DVDs: Although I am not here to review each of the DVDs, I must say that I was so happy to see such well-made instructional DVDs which are useful for those who live in remote areas and have little resource to quality instructors. It is also way better than simply copying moves from YouTube as the dance instructors on the DVD actually explain clearly the step for each, the follower and the leader.

Kadu and Larissa have a complete series for Beginners, Intermediate, Advance, and Super Advance, plus Men's Styling and Ladies' Styling. Also they have online courses for a monthly fee, cheaper than going to a class if again travelling weekly is not feasible. www.kadularissa.com

Xandy Liberato and Evelyn Magyari have one DVD that is targeted to experienced intermediate and advance

dancers. It is a fun challenge for both leaders and followers to master their 8 combinations.

Last but not least the latest DVD is a set by Alisson Sandi and Audrey Isautier for beginner, intermediate, and advance. Again their DVDs have clear instructions, and they are articulate in explaining the steps with particular emphasis on safety for some advance moves.

Useful websites/blogs:
www.brazilianzoukcouncil.com
www.grapevine.dzouk.com
www.zouknation.com
www.zouk-germany.com
www.zouksidedown.wordpress.com
www.zouktheworld.com

Congresses and Festivals: These Zouk events are held all over the world with at least two offered each month in different cities. Usually they last for a long weekend and others can spill to the week after. The bulk of the workshops are held during the day and afternoon followed by social and performance in the evening. Congresses are bigger with more guest artists and usually held at a full-service hotel. Festivals may be run at a dance studio or several different venues throughout the weekend. These may have more limited guest artists. Although this format can be quite overwhelming for the beginner (and some events now include a Beginner Immersion Series) by the end of the third day even the most advanced can only handle so much information from so many different teachers.

These congresses and festivals allow people to take classes, even privates or if lucky enough to also social dance with Zouk teachers they have only seen on Youtube! It is also a great way to network with fellow Zouk instructors, take each other's classes as a professional continuing education, plan new events or collaborations, as well to promote upcoming events or showcasing up-and-coming Zouk artists/teachers/students through performances. At these events, dance shoes and clothing, earrings, accessories are sold. One of the best parts of congresses is the time together with friends who share the same passion. Close friendships are developed making memorable moments for life!

Training venues: Pre-social lessons vary from one venue to the other. Some lessons are arranged to precede an established social, and some teach a mini movement lesson at the middle of the social, while other venues have different group level classes which are followed by a social. Group lessons at a dance studio that are part of a progressive series are more structured and perhaps offered at earlier times of the day for those who do not want to be up late at night.

Private lessons are the most focused for those who want to learn at a quicker pace, those who want to focus on particular step or technique, those who have had dance experience and want a faster pace than a beginner's class, and of course those who have the financial resources to pay for the high prices of private lesson.

Zouk-ation (Zouk + Vacation in Hawaii's Big Island) is an unusual way of immersing into the fundamentals, focusing with only a teacher or two from the same style/philosophy/aesthetic/technique, which avoids confusion and misunderstanding of what needs to be really learned when there are so many teachers at once. This involves over a weeklong stay away, travel, room and board, and training. But the benefits are noticeable, and great improvement and solid understanding of the dance is achieved. Included in the package are 10-12 hours of classes, accommodations for 8-9 nights, island excursions and meals.

www.zoukation.weebly.com

Other Books and Magazines:

The only book on Zouk so far is Mzouk written and published by Daniel Estevez from Spain. Originally in Spanish, it has been translated to English and Portuguese. The book though focuses specifically on M-zouk style of dance that was developed in Majorca, Spain by Master Gege' and continued by Daniel and Leticia Estevez of Spiral Dancers.

A new e-magazine unveiled in October 2014 and dedicated to Zouk, is Zoukology. This was successfully started by Jessica Caro in NYC to give a chance for people to write about Zouk from different perspectives from around the world. The magazine offers interviews, articles by top teachers, zouk experiences at festivals and congresses, as well as articles on hygiene and age issues. www.zoukology.com

Films and Shows:

In 2013, filmmaker, Wilco De Groot, created a documentary on Brazilian Zouk titled *Dance of Love* that follows 4 individuals and how their Zouk dancing brought meaning to their life. It won the California Film Award Grand Prize in 2013 in San Diego.

In 2014, an original show *Brazouka* premiered at the Fringe Festival in the UK. The grand show with an extraordinary International cast of dancers, combines Brazilian Zouk dancing, its history, Afro Brazilian dances, and a passionate story of legendary Lambazouk dancer, Braz Dos Santos written by Pamela Stephenson-Connolly, directed by Arlene Phillips, and narrated by Billy Connolly.

Frequently Asked Question:
How do you find a teacher in the USA?

Social media is the best way to connect you to a teacher near you. Facebook has pages for the various Zouk organizations and groups around the world where you can also ask where one might find an instructor in your particular area. The Zouk Nation has a website, ZoukNation.com and not only does it list instructors but also has some informative articles/interviews. Zoukology a new magazine dedicated to Zouk, has an article http://bit.ly/1JwAZkA on how to get a Zouk community started from zero.

Atlanta: Eddie Bonnell, Adrian Lopez, Atoro, Ebonie Lee;
Austin: Pinaki Ghosh, Favian Buston, Hannah Miller;
Boston: Inna Grant, Edwin Johnson, Glenio Oliveira;
Brooklyn: Ebonie Lee;
Chicago: Sarah Zuccaro, Chris Van Houten, James Bonesho;
Dallas/Fort Worth: Luis Laredo, Emily Ruchaud;
Detroit: Marc Brewer;
Knoxville: Brad Meccia, Ian Orr;
Honolulu: Kimberly Loo (Honolulu Zouk), Geebin Mak and
        Jonathan Troupe (Island Zouk);
Houston: Vivian Nguyen, George Ozoude, Alma Guevara;
Los Angeles: Tirso Chauca, Shani Meyer, Christina Montoya,
        Ivo Viera, Lena Thieme, Ryan Wong, Mea-Lynn Wong;
Miami: Kendra Haynes, Natalie Savage, Raheem Maliki, Jon Malave,
        Navon Wallace;
Milwaukee: James Bonesho;
New York: Aline Cleto, Shelby Joy Cole, Shannon Cronyn,
        Charles Espinosa, Igor Fraga, Ronny Soares Dutra,
        Hisako Izutsu, Jessica Lamdon, Clo Fereira, Rodrigo Ramalho,
        Jeremey Adam Rey, Kim Rottier, Juni Shimitzu,
        Henry velandia (Ry'el);
Orlando: Kendra Haynes;
Princeton: Clo Ferreira, Kevin Toft, Henry velandia (Ry'el);
Portland: Nathalia Carbajal;
Raleigh: Christian Melo, Rachel Meth;
Sacramento: Joel Beall;
Seattle: Xtine, Elizabeth Burnett, Robert Luu, Kelsey Rote;
San Diego: Philip Miha, Kelly Rice, Fabiola Gomez;
San Francisco: Annita Chinita Lambadeira,
        Nicolas Nelsom Susan Rebellon, Girish ZK;
Tampa: Kendra Haynes;
Washington, D.C.: Bianca Dag Dee, Ashley Kent, Sami Selo,
        Amy White;

Last but not least: Big Island of Hawai'i (towns of Kona, Waimea, Holualoa, Hilo, and Captain Cook): Marie Alonzo Snyder, Stephanie Bolton.

ZOUK HI

As I teach the dance more each week, I am slowly falling deeply in love with the dance, not only for the exquisite feeling I experience dancing it, but for being able to share that feeling with others. Indeed, with my academic experience and my background in dance education, the first Zouk HI Teacher Training Course is scheduled for 2016. This carefully designed course, offers an integrated and creative Zouk teacher training program to help dance teachers bring solid Zouk fundamentals to their communities.

It is thrilling to see Brazilian people come to class who have never heard of Zouk in their country, enjoying the dance and wanting more. It is inspiring to see women giving themselves that gift of dance and learn about their bodies, their emotions, and their connection through dancing. It brings me great joy to see quiet and shy men now enjoying the dance, and encouraging and helping others learn the dance.

It is fascinating to see musicians, woodworkers, dancers, painters, students, construction workers, yogis, chefs, realtors, teachers, and paramedics coming together and finding that common ground with their dancing. And lastly, it is empowering for all to simply be in the company of people who want to learn and be challenged, who want to connect, and who want to enjoy life through dance.

Frequently Asked Question:
What is in the future for Zouk on the Big Island?

There is so much potential for expansion and growth in this island. A social completely dedicated to Zouk would be an awesome goal. Some Keiki Zouk for the youth as a physical activity, human connection and social activity away from technology. A dance team for performances around the island would help promote the dance, and give a nice challenge for the more advanced students. More Zouk-ation opportunities with different levels. Within the first year the Big Island had the opportunity to bring outstanding professional and skilled teachers like Jeremey Adam Rey of rawZouk from NYC and Solange Dias of Zouklambada UK from London.

Hopefully with more people that now know Zouk, more International Zouk masters will choose the Big Island of Hawai'i for a vacation spot and combine the cultural experience with master dance workshops. Last but not least, perhaps a unique festival that will bring together Hula, Zouk, West Coast Swing, Modern Dance, Belly Dance, and Pole Dance/Art and create a fertile exchange of techniques, teaching styles, and continued professional development in dance.

(*Photo by Irina Ulanova*)

CONCLUSION

What I learned from social dancing like Zouk is that dance brings so much joy in people's lives. Through dance some people feel empowered: they feel free, they feel they have permission to be sexy, they feel re-energized, they feel happy--basically all the results from endorphins! But what really has impressed me is that we, as humans, seem to need this kind of socialization and contact especially in this generation that relies too much on technology for those aspects in life. I also found that this passion for dancing is equal to that of trained and professional dancers.

Dance is simply part of all cultures and subcultures in our society because it completes the individual. Through dance we each bring a moment of beauty, between two people, that is almost sacred. Within that one song, two people have the capability to create a magical moment with their delicious dancing. And at the end of the dance, we keep being reminded that dance is a basic human activity like no other, it is primal in our being.

So when we see T-shirts that say *I'm Zouk, Zouk me, Zouk you, Got Zouk?, Keep Calm and Zouk on, Hug me if you Zouk*, or my favorite *I know how to Zouk, what is your Super Power* -, those are simply invitations to connect, it is already the beginning of the dance. And for that moment when two individuals decide to dance they transcend race, age, class, income level, education, disabilities, sexual orientation, body image, religion, and at times gender. With Zouk, we break the boundaries that separate us and, for that one song, we come together and invite, listen and connect with aloha.

REFERENCES

1 music, 3 couples, 3 styles-ZoukdoBrazil.fr, Paris 2015 http://tinyurl.com/o7vqmjd

Adilio Porto www.zouknation.net http://tinyurl.com/l9vm5ff

Bamboo, N. History of Zouk in NYC 2015(Unpublished)

Béhague, Gerard The Lundu and Modinha of Brazil in the Nineteenth Century http://tinyurl.com/o274yqe

Brazilian Zouk in Finland http://tinyurl.com/pz4v224

Cadence Rampa https://en.wikipedia.org/wiki/Cadence_rampa

Céline, Gaëlle ZoukSide Down – A journey with Brazilian Zouk www. zouksidedown.wordpress.com

Coladeira http://en.wikipedia.org/wiki/Coladeira#The_cola-zouk

Compas http://en.wikipedia.org/wiki/Compas

Dança do Carimbó-Belém–Pará http://tinyurl.com/lyzk4ew

Dance: Poetry in Movement http://tinyurl.com/klz6ztu

De Carvalho, Alex http://tinyurl.com/ooprqxo

Etiquette Brazilian Zouk http://tinyurl.com/pgtw3yf

History of Lambada Dance www.dancelessons.net http://tinyurl.com/pbpq4lu

Izutsu, H. Conversations on Zouk history in NYC/USA 10/23/2013

Joe uchôa e Laura Vieira-Dança Lundu e Carimbó http://tinyurl.com/m3hu7uy

kassav' apré zouk la (live) http://tinyurl.com/ngkaxlk

Lundu marajoara http://tinyurl.com/ldsxaqc

Marajo´ Island http://gobrazil.about.com/od/brazilianbeachesislands/a/marajo.htm

REFERENCES

Maxixe http://en.wikipedia.org/wiki/Maxixe_(dance)

Renata Pecanha & Jorge Peres, www.russianzoukcongress.com

Lundu marajoara http://tinyurl.com/ldsxaqc

Marajo´ Island http://gobrazil.about.com/od/brazilianbeachesislands/a/marajo.htm

Maxixe http://en.wikipedia.org/wiki/Maxixe_(dance)

Renata Pecanha & Jorge Peres, www.russianzoukcongress.com

Rottier, K. What is Brazilian Zouk www.zouknewyork.com

The history of ZOUK & Lambada http://tinyurl.com/pv3plfu

The meaning behind Aloha https://www.youtube.com/watch?v=nG6LoTxqEaM

The story of Braz Dos Santos www.brazlambazouk.com http://tinyurl.com/kr2tojt

Understanding different phases and styles www.brazilianzoukcouncil.com http://tinyurl.com/ndh5eom

ZenZouk www.zenzouk.com

Zouk www.heritageinstitute.com http://tinyurl.com/pswjww6

Zouk http://en.wikipedia.org/wiki/Zouk

Zouk-ation ... intensive zouk workshop with Jeremey Adam Rey http://tinyurl.com/kzzg6cs

Zouk dance of the Caribbean http://tinyurl.com/n7sdynf

Zouk Lambada http://en.wikipedia.org/wiki/Zouk-Lambada

Zouk Music & Videos http://tinyurl.com/mpnlu4h

Zouk the Dance of Love–trailer http://tinyurl.com/prgdjnr

Chronological Chart
Development of Zouk Lambada Dance from Porto Seguro

1549   Pedro Alvares Cadral Portuguese landed in Porto Seguro and claimed territory for Portugal

17th century   Beginning of Colonization in Para Brazil, Carimbo' involved only side to side movements and many spins and hip movement, two beat rhythm with tall drum

18th century   Lundu Afro-Brazilian song and dance brought by Bantu slaves from Angola, some considered as witch craft

1749   Brazilian musician Manuel de Almeida Botelho immigrated to Lisbon bringing Lundu

            Lundu's sexualized quality is attractive to Europeans in Brazil

            The reigns of Dom Jose I (1750-77), Dona Maria I (1777-92)
            Lundu song and dance popular with Elite group in Brazil the doce lundum chorado (sweet crying lundu)

19th century   Lundu century's musical choice of Luso-Brazilian bourgeoisie—dance was flirtatious ritual couple dance became salon dance

            Choro Brazilian musicians to European musical styles

            Polish Mazurka (Mazouk) introduced in French Caribbean

1845   Polka arrived in Rio fusing with African rhythms, principally the Lundu

1868   Maxixe from Rio De Janeiro also known as Brazilian Tango-fusion of Afro-Brazilian dance Lundu and European Polka. Early development of Boneca and Apagado

20th century   Lundu dance faded but song survived with more melodic and romantic tone

            Maxixe reached Europe

1920   Maxixe Spicy lyrics and movement—true Forbidden Dance

Chronological Chart
Development of Zouk Lambada Dance from Porto Seguro

1976	Brazilian composer Pinduca launched song Lambada (sembao)
1978	Master Veira launched record Lambada of Quebradas
1980	Carimbo' music fused with new developing Caribbean music (from North-East of Brazil with influence of tourist) and called Lambada the dance and the music
1980	Lambada dance and music spreads in coast of Brazil and reaches Porto Seguro
1981	Song "Llorando se fue" by Bolivian group Los Kjarkas. Original song of Lambada later translated in Portuguese.
1983	Carimbo' and Lundu still being danced as couple in Marajo´ Island
1986	"Chorango se fue" translated and released in Márcia Ferreira 3rd album and by José Ari
1988	Carnival of Bahia, Lambada became popular and found its home in Porto Seguro
	Olivier Lamotte d'Incamps, French producer, created band Kaoma bought rights to 300 Lambada songs
	Braz and Didi dos Santos developed LambaZouk while touring with Kaoma
1990	Kaoma release "Lambada" a song they plagiarized from Ferreira which became a big hit all over the world Hermosa brothers (authors), Márcia Ferreira (translation), José Ari (translation), and Alberto Maravi (original producer)
	Movies: Lambada; The Forbidden Dance; Lambada (Brazilian film)
	Adilio Porto and Renata Peçanha dancers with Jaime Aroxa develop Rio Zouk/Zouk Love
1994	Lambada music fades other music is used for the dance, one of them was Caribbean Zouk * or Kompas
2007	Mafie Zouker introduced remix and developed new style Neo Zouk giving way to Zouk Flow, Soul Zouk, Zouk R & B
2013	Contemporary Zouk increased use of modern dance techniques and of Classical or contemporary music some without clear Rio Zouk beat

Chronological Chart
INTERSECTION OF CARIBBEAN ZOUK MUSIC & DANCE

19th century   Polish Mazurka (Mazouk) is introduced French Caribbean islands (Guadalupe, Martinique, St. Martin, St. Barthelemy, French Guiana, Haiti, Dominica, St. Lucia)

1955   Konpa/Compa music genre and modern meringue from Haiti–close partnering with movements from hips

1962   Kadans/Cadence Rampa/Kadans Ranpa or modern méringue popularized in the Caribbean by the virtuoso Haitian sax player Webert Sicot

1960-70   French Antilles (Guadalupe, St. Martin, Martinique, St. Barthelemy) becomes replete with Kadans bands

1970-80   Zouk meaning party or festival in Creole, zouk word originally from zouke, sekwe, zouke, etc. from the French verb "secouer" meaning "shake intensely and repeatedly" fast carnival beat style music and dance from Guadalupe and Martinique

1978   French producer Pierre Edouard Decimus and brother Georges Decimus with Guadeloupean Jacob Desvarieux to Internationalize Kadans

1979   Kassav band was created by Decimus brothers took Konpa/Compa to many places

1980   Kizomba music developed in Angola with influence of Konpas/Compas from French Caribbean

Kassav band with MIDI technology (Musical Instrument Digital Interface) added to Zouk, Konpas/Compas, and Kadans

1984   Latin American hit by Kassav with Yélélé,

1994   Lambada music fades and other music is used for the Lambada dance, one of them was Caribbean Zouk or Konpas /Compas

21st century   Zouk or zouk-love is the French Antilles Kadans or Konpas/Compas

About The Author

Marie Alonzo Snyder is the founder and artistic director of Tangerine Dance Collective www.tangerinedance.com, a modern dancer, choreographer, scholar and educator. Born in the Philippines, Marie was raised in Italy and eventually settled in New York City attending New York University's Tisch School of the Arts earning her BFA and MFA in Dance.

Since 1986 Marie's works have been presented in New York, Princeton and throughout the United States, Canada, Philippines and England. Marie is a founding member of the West Windsor Arts Council, which helped convert an old Firehouse into the West Windsor Arts Center, in NJ and in 2004 she co-founded the "I'll have what she's having…" Dance Project, a dance cooperative of NJ 40Up women choreographers.

Marie also earned her EdD from Teachers College, Columbia University. Also a certified Classical Pilates, American DanceWheels Foundation and ZoukNY instructor, Marie was on the faculty of Princeton Dance and Theater Studio and an adjunct at The College of New Jersey. Marie was the Program Director for DanceVision (now Princeton Youth Ballet). She has facilitated the collaboration with The Parkinson Alliance in bringing to the community Princeton Dance for Parkinson's, a special class for people with Parkinson's Disease.

Marie started her Zouk training in 2011 studying with Jeremey Adam Rey, Solange Dias, K-Yo Victor, Evelyn Magyari, Xandi Liberato, Kim Rottier, Larissa Thayane, Henry velandia (Ry'el), Daniela Pascual, Cledson Gomes, Getulio Ramalho, Ronny Dutra, Bruno Cura, Rodrigo Ramalho, and as many teachers at Congresses and Festivals.

Lately she has been exploring other dances to keep challenging herself physically and artistically by studying Belly Dance with Stephanie Bolton, Pole Art/Fitness with Almitra Karastan and Hula with Kumu Keala Ching. Marie moved to the Big Island of Hawai'i in November 2014 and is teaching Brazilian Zouk in Kona, Holualoa, Waimea, UH Hilo and Captain Cook, as well as teaching Pilates at The Club in Kona.

(logo by Fuki Funakoshi)

Zouk-Inspired Drinks

Zouking at spacious bar venues is prevalent in the Zouk community. It is a way to promote the dance with some lessons at the beginning and a social right after. It is also a way for the bar to have an event that will bring people traffic, especially during the weekdays. In London, at the Grace Bar on Monday nights, you can catch classes with Solange Dias and Joe Koniak. In New York on Tuesdays at Solas, in the East Village, you will find various New York City Zouk teachers and visiting instructors teaching a lesson before the dancing begins. Similarly, on Tuesdays, in downtown Kona, Hawai'i at Daylight Mind, one can enjoy the beautiful breeze of the ocean while dancing or sipping some Zouk-inspired cocktails. These were created by Tina Maxwell, a bartender, who was inspired by the dancing. Here are her delicious and refreshing concoctions worthy of their names!

ZoukaTina

2 oz. tequila
1/2 oz. of lychee purée
1/2 oz. of grapefruit juice

Shake with ice and served martini style with li hing mui rimmed glasses

Bonecarita

2 sprigs of lavender
2 springs of mint,
2 lime wedges
Muddle ingredients
2 oz. tequila
2 oz. homemade sour mix
Shake
Serve over ice with li hing mui rimmed glasses